Songs

IN THE

Night

When
and
Hope is Fleeting

To
Carol Ann
God Bless
You
Pamela Goss

Pamela Goss

Printed in Canada

Print ISBN: 978-1-4866-1841-5
eBook ISBN: 978-1-4866-1842-2

Word Alive Press
119 De Baets Street, Winnipeg, MB R2J 3R9
www.wordalivepress.ca

Cataloguing in Publication may be obtained through Library and Archives Canada

To Hilary Tyne and Mary-Martha McRae, for encouraging
me to persevere in life, as well as in my writing, and for
inspiring me to be so much more than I ever imagined.

Contents

Acknowledgements

Thank you to author Judi Peers, who first edited my book and encouraged me to continue. To my husband John for all the computer assistance. To all those at Word Alive Press for bringing my book to fruition.

All photos are the author's except for the one featured on Day Twelve by José Saenz and Day Twenty-Two by Stephanie Goss.

Introduction

In a second, in a heartbeat, the unexpected happens and our lives are changed, shaken to the very core. Often it's something we thought would never happen to us or those we love. We are broadsided, like it or not. Realizing that we aren't in control can be devastating. We pray for a miracle, but God says, "My grace is sufficient for you." We have no choice but to go on.

Good news: we have One who will come alongside and help us through, One who can strengthen and empower us to not only survive but be victorious.

When I was a baby, I contracted polio, which mostly damaged my feet and legs. When I was thirty, I was struck with post-polio syndrome, which meant more weakness and chronic pain. I have undergone many surgeries to keep me walking. As both a mom and foster mom, who cares for many children, I have found that I have a God who supports and sustains me. I feel joy when I walk through this journey with Jesus.

Let this book of thirty-one prayers, inspired by the Psalms, comfort, encourage, and strengthen you during your times of great trial. As you offer praise amidst the pain, God will come alongside you. You'll find your fear being transformed into trust, your doubt to faith, your trembling to confidence. You will have hope to face whatever the day may bring and come to know that you're being held in the loving, capable hands of the Lord.

They are strong, like a tree planted by a river. The tree produces fruit in season, and its leaves don't die. Everything they do will succeed.

—Psalm 1:3

Rest and Renewal

Lord, you are my resting place, my haven, when I get weary and everything drags me down. As I turn to you, I am renewed and my heart fills with joy!

My creator God, as I listen to the lapping of the water, see the sparkling sun on the lake, and gaze up at the majestic mountains all around, I am filled with a sense of wonder and peace floods my soul. My God, you created all this. You are the One who helps and watches over me always.

As I contemplate my life, I can see how you have been there for me. Praise bubbles up. Many times I have seen you do things in my life that can't be easily explained, like the time you healed my six-month-old daughter of the lump in her throat. The doctors were baffled when they went to surgically remove it and it was gone, but I knew it was your touch, a miracle. Hallelujah!

You chose me and I am yours, a child of the King, your princess. How fabulous is that, to be joint-heirs with Jesus, to have everlasting life in a place prepared by you! I cannot begin to imagine what that will be like. I wait in joyful anticipation, my Jesus.

In your great name I pray, amen.

You will teach me how to live a holy life. Being with you will fill me with joy; at your right hand I will find pleasure forever.

—Psalm 16:11

Pamela Goss

DAY TWO
Hand in Hand

Jesus, I offer up praise to you for your abundant blessings on my life. Thank you for the godly people who are part of my life, for they encourage and inspire me to go higher, to be more and do more than I ever thought I could.

I am thankful for my pleasant life, with beauty all around me. On this cold winter day, the sun warms me through the window, like a hug from you. It's like being wrapped in your arms of love. Wrap your arms around my friends as well, for they are precious to me. Pour out your blessings on them this day. I know they are a gift, enriching my life. They are kindred spirits to journey with on my path.

You are the friend who never leaves me. Reach down and take hold of my hand and I will walk with you today, step by step. Together we will handle whatever comes. You are my rock and my fortress, my stronghold, my deliverer, and my shield. You are the One who sustains me and helps me through. Even in the midst of a storm, I have peace, for you are my hiding place, my strong tower. There is no better friend than you.

In Jesus name, my friend, amen.

The Lord is my shepherd; I have everything I need.

—Psalm 23:1

Pamela Goss

DAY THREE
I Will Follow Him

My Lord, my shepherd, I am yours, for you care for me as a shepherd cares for his sheep. You lead and guide me, providing for all my needs. You love me so completely that I surrender my all to you.

With a joyful spirit, I will serve you. As I follow your lead, blessings will follow. What an adventure it is living for you! You know my heart, my dreams, and my plans.

I pray that you will give me the desires of my heart. Your plan for my life is to prosper me and not to harm me, to do me good. So I pray that all my steps are headed in the right direction, for that is where my joy and victory will come. My heartfelt prayer is, "Thy will be done."

My merciful Father, thank you for your continued grace. When I have overburdened myself, you have come along and made me rest in order that I can be refreshed once again. How wonderful it is to have a shepherd who anticipates my every need and intervenes in a way that is best for me.

So help me keep my priorities right, not seeking fame and fortune and only doing what has eternal value. With my life in your hands, I can say "No worries."

I am yours, my loving Father. Amen.

Who is this glorious King? The Lord All-Powerful—he is the glorious King.

—Psalm 24:10

Pamela Goss

Glorious and Free

Oh Lord God Almighty, the King of Glory, so strong and mighty, I seek your face today. Who is on the Lord's side? I am, now and forever. So I pray for courage to stand up for you and for what is right, to speak up when I need to.

My heart hurts for all the suffering I see. So many bad things are happening. People's good moral values are falling apart, and they are hurting others with great delight. But a day of reckoning is coming and you will deal with all of this in perfect justice.

Lord, give me a passion to do what is right and honest, no matter what the cost is to me. I want to bring honour and glory to you by the way I treat others. Help me to always act in the best interests of others, for then I will be acting in love.

Please give us leaders who will turn to you for wisdom and have the courage to stand up for what's right. I place my country in your hands. I trust in you, for you have answered and protected and saved me when I called to you. I lift up my banner and shout for joy, for we live in a land that is glorious and free.

To you be all the glory, amen.

The Lord is my strength and shield. I trust him, and he helps me. I am very happy, and I praise him with my song.

—Psalm 28:7

Pamela Goss

His Hands

Lord, please bend your ear to me and listen to my cries for help. I am living in obedience and striving to do right, but so often I mess up. Please forgive and help me to forgive myself. Fear and remorse and self-loathing bring me down, so I pray for restoration, for joy and gladness to fill my heart again. My precious Saviour, create in me a clean heart and renew a right spirit within me. You, my Redeemer, make all things new.

I need not have any fear, for you are my strong tower, my refuge. I am so thankful to have you in my life, for guidance and protection. This is security, to know you are ultimately in control. I place my life in your all-powerful hands.

I go forward with peace because you are fulfilling your plans and purposes for my life. Nothing happens accidentally. You will never leave me or forsake me, and I will do more than just make it through; I will overcome. You are my rock and so I stand upon you in triumph. Oh my precious Father, my heart sings as I lift my hands in praise, for you have given me the victory. My heart leaps with joy. Eternal praises to you, my God and my King.

With a thankful heart, amen.

The Lord gives strength to his people; the Lord blesses his people with peace.
—Psalm 29:11

Pamela Goss

Eye of the Storm

Oh God, such a thunderstorm! Flashes of lightning pierce the sky and thunder booms and crashes. I feel like the storm is my life right now, closing in on me. I remember the prayer I prayed as a child: "Dear God, I'm sailing on thy wide, wide sea. Please guide my little ship for me." As an adult, I still need your guidance and direction. Either calm my stormy seas or show me how to ride the waves and handle the winds.

You are my lighthouse, guiding me, when the way is hard to see. I know you will bring me to a safe harbour even if it means taking me home to heaven, for there is a time to die and I know I will go when my work on earth is done.

I trust you with my life and the ones I dearly love. Your love and truth are with me wherever I go. Persevering, I will make it through with your hand in mine. I am a winner, an overcomer, and I can be victorious no matter what. Lord, I love my life here, but it would be even better to be with you. I am in a win-win situation.

Thank you for being with me no matter what. What a Saviour! I love you, Lord, and give you all the praise!

In Jesus name, amen.

How great is your goodness that you have stored up for those who fear you, that you have given to those who trust you. You do this for all to see.
—Psalm 31:19

Pamela Goss

A Gift to Enjoy

L ord, today I am going to head to the beach because it's a windy day, my favourite, sent by you as a gift to enjoy. I love the huge waves crashing against the shore and the wind blowing my hair. It is so loud and powerful. But you are so much more powerful and majestic. You stand forever as my rock, my hiding place. In your goodness and mercy, you have set my feet in a spacious place. You set me free because you love me unfailingly. I praise you for showing me such wonderful love. You give me strength and hope.

When so many troubles come down on me, I say, "I wish I had the wings of a dove. Then I would fly away and rest." I feel the world pushing against me from all sides. I am hard-pressed, but not crushed. I know, Lord, that you use every difficulty to confide deep things to me. I grow so strong through these times, and this is when you give your greatest gifts. I trust you, for you never let me down. You are my rock, and on my rock I stand.

In my strengthener's name, amen.

Are there those who respect the Lord? He will point them to the best way. They will enjoy a good life, and their children will inherit the land.

—Psalm 25:12–13

Pamela Goss

A Reflection of Jesus

I pray, Jesus, that my life will bring honour to you. May others see a reflection of you in my life. Help me, Lord, not to lie, gossip, or be dishonest in any way. Today I want to spend time with you. I want to learn your ways, for you are good and righteous.

I know you are loving and true and help me to act in love towards others. Forgive me, Jesus, for I have failed in this so often lately. Sometimes my biggest enemy is myself and I so easily fall into the trap of wrong thinking and acting. Help me to keep my eyes focused on you and my mind filled with good thoughts. Lord, may I bring forth fruit on this day so those around me will want to taste and see that you are good. It is good to tell others of the many ways in which you show me love, and this just proves how deep your thoughts are towards me. You never fail me.

I thank you for my good friends who help me along, building me up. They are there for me through the tough times and make life fun, giving me the gift of laughter. Lord, by your grace, I want to enjoy my life to the fullest, this abundant life you died to give me. I choose joy!

In your righteous name, my Jesus, amen.

The Lord says, "I will make you wise and show you where to go. I will guide you and watch over you."

—Psalm 32:8

Pamela Goss

Make My Life Count

L ord, I want my life to really count. I don't want to flounder around, missing your plans for my life. Life is so busy and it's easy to get caught up in it all, so please help me this day to not miss those opportunities you send my way. Help me to focus on others and not be so self-absorbed.

In following you, I know my life will be blessed and full of meaning. Real joy will come as I seek to fulfill your purpose. Please forgive my sins, as I don't want there to be anything between us. With my sins forgiven, I can go forward in confidence knowing that your unfailing love surrounds me wherever I go. With you as my defender, Lord, I am unshakeable. You are my rock and my salvation.

My Father, today I'm struggling with disappointment and sorrow, so open my eyes and my heart to see something wonderful. All around I see your gifts of beauty, insight, and love. As my eyes are opened, I will offer them back to you as a thanks offering. Help me to focus on all I do have, to live this day fully, with joy and expectation.

In your name I pray, amen.

Examine and see how good the Lord is. Happy is the person who trusts him.
—Psalm 34:8

Pamela Goss

DAY TEN
His Healing Touch

My God who heals me, I live in a broken world and I too am broken. God, I need your healing touch today, for I am very ill. In your great mercy, heal me, for I trust and look to you for my support. I feel like I am in a cave of despair, robbing me of any joy. Tears stream down my face as I cry out to you.

Free me from this depression and I will praise your name and enjoy life once again. I don't see how you can use this time, but I trust that you will bring good out of it. There is a master plan for my life.

You alone can satisfy my deepest needs and sustain me through this trial. Disappointment won't be mine when I put my trust in you, for there is a greater purpose that isn't always obvious to me. Give me the grace to bear this. Come near to me and heal my broken heart. Give me patience, Lord, as I wait for your perfect timing and perfect answer to my needs, in all ways.

I see your goodness when you go beyond my needs and fulfill my heart's desire like a beautifully wrapped gift just waiting to be opened, sent from your heart of love. My heart fills with hope and I wait with expectation, my Lord.

In your precious name, amen.

Those people honor me who bring me offerings to show thanks. And I, God, will save those who do that.

—Psalm 50:23

Pamela Goss

Thank Offerings

God, today I want to offer thank offerings to you. Thank you for all you do for me each day. Thank you for financial help just when I need it, for prompting a friend to call, for sending someone new into my life, for days filled with purpose and for my spouse who is my best friend. Thank you for helping us when we don't know what to do. Thank you even when the news is not good, for I know you will give me what I need to handle it. Thank you for all your TLC of me.

Lord, I have a new song to sing, one of joy and victory. Thank you for your loyalty and for saving me and transforming my life so that my inward beauty shines through. Help me to keep my mind fixed on true and praiseworthy things. Let beautiful thoughts fill my mind.

Lord, saying thank you just doesn't seem to be enough. You have saved me and pulled me up. You have set me free from the bondage I and others have chained me up with. I will not believe those lies anymore, for they are from the pit of hell. I am yours and I want to serve you all my days out of my deep love and devotion to you. Here are my thank offerings to you. My heart is forever yours.

In my Saviour's name, amen.

He sends help from heaven and saves me. He punishes those who chase me. . . God sends me his love and truth.

—Psalm 57:3

Pamela Goss

DAY TWELVE
The Great Defender

Jesus, I am hurting today, for I am being falsely accused and attacked. What's worse is that it's someone I love. But of course you know what this feels like, so I give it over to you. Please vindicate me, for you know me, and bless my accuser.

If you are for me, who could ever be against me and succeed? Their words are as sharp as a lion's teeth. Hide me in the shadow of your wings, God Most High. I will trust in your love and faithfulness, and I know you will deal out justice.

You are my perfect defender. I feel like I'm being torn apart and I pray for your protection. Cover me with your shield and rescue me. You are a just God. What fools are they who have no fear of you!

Even in the midst of all this, I know you are with me, lighting the way for me. I have joy and peace, so that I can still enjoy my life, no matter what. I praise your name and your greatness and will tell others how good you are to me. All praise to you, the rock on which I stand. Be exalted, O God, and let your glory shine!

In my great defender's name, amen.

I stay close to you; you support me with your right hand.

—Psalm 63:8

Pamela Goss

DAY THIRTEEN

Satisfaction Guaranteed

Jesus, you satisfy me completely as I spend time with you and search out truths from the Bible. Help me today to keep my thoughts on what I read this morning. It is a jewel to carry with me all day.

There is so much I have to handle, and today is a bad pain day for me. Please support me with your right hand, which flows with your unlimited power into me, supplying me fully with all that I need to make it through.

I praise you, oh my precious Jesus. You are the one who has turned the tide of my feelings of emptiness and hopelessness to a heart full of songs of joy. There is no one like my God who reaches down and touches me and I am made whole.

Lord, your word is so precious to me; I live by it and hope in it. It is truth, and I love your teachings. It is a treasure to search out and find the precious gems hidden there. I rest on your promises to me. It is my comfort through these hard times.

To me, Jesus, you are my hiding place and my shield. You fill up all the deep hunger I have inside and I am totally devoted to you. I am yours and I am satisfied.

With a grateful heart, amen.

But I am always with you; you have held my hand. You guide me with your advice, and later you will receive me in honor.

—Psalm 73:23–24

Pamela Goss

DAY FOURTEEN
There Is More

W hy, Lord, do those who live for themselves and have no interest in you seem to prosper? But when looking at it from an eternal viewpoint, I see that this life will be over in a moment and then they will face eternal destruction if they don't know you as their Saviour! It breaks my heart to see those I care about lost, so please open their eyes to the truth. As far as the east is from the west, my sins have been forgiven by your grace. My choice to accept your free gift means that I have no fear of death, for I am saved for all eternity.

I know, too, that nothing happens in my life by accident, that everything happens for a purpose—and best of all, for my good. Real riches come from being a child of the King, from being lovingly cared for as you meet my needs.

This world will one day answer to God, and every knee will bow. Now is the time. My heart rejoices, for my future is going to be more than I could ever have hoped for. Jesus is preparing a mansion for me in heaven.

Your Father's heart just loves to bless us. So, too, may I bless others unselfishly, as my heart overflows with love.

In your loving name, Jesus, amen.

Lord All-Powerful, happy are the people who trust you!

—Psalm 84:12

Pamela Goss

Unlimited Power

Lord, I am strong in you. You are my rock, my shield, and my protection against my enemies. I love you. There is no one holy like my God, who is worthy to be praised. When troubled waters were about to cover my head, you reached down and pulled me to safety. It's such a marvellous thing that the Most High God takes delight in me and saves me. With your help, Father, I can make it through anything. I will be victorious and do what is right. I trust you with my life. Support me, Lord, with your powerful right hand.

Lord God All-Powerful, I am passing through the valley of weeping and I know you are transforming it into blessings. No matter what, I would rather spend one day in your house than a thousand elsewhere. My soul yearns to spend time with you, and one day I will see you face to face. My citizenship is in heaven and I am just passing through this earthly life. Oh what a day that will be!

I come to worship you, to meditate on your great love for me. You are so great, so all-powerful, that I need never live in fear. You are my God, forever. Praise the Lord!

In my all-powerful Jesus name, amen.

Love and truth belong to God's people; goodness and peace will be theirs.
—Psalm 85:10

Pamela Goss

DAY SIXTEEN
Forgiveness

Lord, I feel like a failure, for I have allowed my sinful nature to take control and my sin is weighing heavily on me. It makes me physically sick and spiritually weak. It comes between us.

Please forgive me for my sins. I confess them to you and ask your forgiveness. Against you, and you alone, have I sinned. I have hurt you by my actions. Thoughtlessly, I have gone astray and now I pray for a willing and obedient spirit. Lord, I want to know again the joy of fellowship with you. Cleanse me and renew me, my Redeemer. If I need to change something in my life, show me and I will do it. Create in me a pure heart, oh God, and because you are rich in mercy, restore me once again.

Lord, as I seek to know you and spend time with you, reveal yourself to me. Love and truth, goodness and peace are mine. These are the true riches of this life. Your goodness shines down from heaven and I am so blessed. As I enjoy sweet fellowship again, my heart overflows with love for you, my Jesus.

Lord, I thank you with all my heart for your goodness. Your Father's heart desires my company. Even when I mess up, you are merciful and forgiving. I sing eternal praises.

In my great Redeemer's name, amen.

Lord, you are kind and forgiving and have great love for those who call to you.

—Psalm 86:5

Pamela Goss

You Raise Me Up

Oh my faithful Lord, please vindicate me. I trust you, without wavering, to do right by me. You know my heart and mind. It hurts to be falsely accused, but I know I am innocent. Please, I look to you for deliverance. How great is your love for me! I lift up my soul to you. How faithful you are to hear and answer when I call.

God, you are so awesome to do the things you do. You alone are worthy of my total devotion and worship. All glory be to you. You raise me up to handle all my trials. Your joy is my strength. I can face everything, because you strengthen and help me. I am not alone and will not fear, for you are my strong tower, my rock. I will endure. Even more, you will bring good out of other people's intended harm.

Lord, you will lift me up and set me free. I am blessed, for I trust in you. As long as I live, I will sing praises to you, my God. Eternal praises be to my Lord and King, the all-powerful, omnipotent One. You are sovereign, almighty, and glorious. One day, all will bow the knee. What a glorious day that will be!

In Jesus name, amen.

Teach us how short our lives really are so that we may be wise.

—Psalm 90:12

Pamela Goss

Wisdom in Perfect Supply

In your unfailing love for me, pour out your blessings so that I am restored and strengthened and healthy to do all you have for me this day.

Thankfully, your mercies are new every morning and you will give me sufficient grace to handle today. In your hands of love and compassion, I will make it through. I need you now, Lord, and even though the way seems dark and obstructed from my view, you see clearly. So take my hand and we will face this together. When it is over, I will be amazed to see that I have been changed in ways I never dreamed. My circumstances are horrendous right now, but with your help I can face this trial with peace in my soul, for this I have Jesus.

On this journey, may I be flexible enough to help someone else and not be self-centred. May I have the wisdom to say no when someone asks something that isn't from you. I pray for insight to see the needs of others I come in contact with today. Our lives are but a moment of time, just as a day is like a thousand years to you, so help me live for eternity, to spend my life on things that matter. May my life bring glory to you as your ambassador.

In your glorious name, Jesus, amen.

But the Lord is my defender; my God is the rock of my protection.

—Psalm 94:22

Pamela Goss

Under Attack

Lord, when I felt those bitter words slung my way, they were like arrows piercing my heart with pain. My God, you see into my heart and know my motives, so I look to you for protection. What others don't realize is that by attacking me, they are taking you on, the God of the universe. I am confident, because you are my defender, the rock of my protection. How safe is that! You are a righteous judge and you will do right.

May those who have attacked me come to know you as I do. They are missing so much. Oh Lord, I don't want them to face eternity without you. Work in their lives and let their hearts be softened and their eyes opened to let you in. Just as you have completely forgiven me, I forgive them. You show me so much love every day and meet my deepest needs so that I can be forgiving to others. Help them, Lord, as you have helped me.

Bless me as I strive to live for you. Nothing is worth letting unforgiveness separate you and me. I praise your name, for you are merciful. Because I forgive others totally, I am free to have abundant joy and the peace that passes all understanding.

With a thankful heart, amen.

A light shines in the dark for honest people, for those who are merciful and kind and good.

—Psalm 112:4

Pamela Goss

DAY TWENTY
No Worries

God, you are holy and I trust you totally with my life. I look up to you, and on you I depend. I know that by following your will for my life, I will have true happiness. Help me to be honest in all my ways. It's like a light shining in the darkness for others to see.

I want to be thought of as a generous person, and it all comes from you, for you give me the ability to produce wealth so that I can give freely.

With you in my life, I need never be afraid of the future. I place myself in your good care.

I have victory over worry. I am victorious, an overcomer. Out of your unfailing love for me, you reached down with your right hand and saved me. You brought me out of a very dark pit. I am made new, a new creature in Christ, and I will never be the same again.

My Lord, may my life bring glory to you in all ways. This is such a special time, spent alone with you. It is a time for renewal, to just be still and listen for your voice. As I look out at the beautiful sunset, I feel happy and at peace. My heart fills with praise. Oh how I love you.

With a heart full of thankfulness, in Jesus name I pray, amen.

He turned a rock into a pool of water, a hard rock into a spring of water.
—Psalm 114:8

Pamela Goss

DAY TWENTY-ONE
Strength to Go On

Dear Jesus, my grief is consuming me and I need your help to persevere.

Lord, you are all-powerful and nothing is impossible to you. In your great kindness, mercy, and love, please save me. Infuse me with your strength, God. In fact, you will never leave me or forsake me, and your arm is not too short to save.

How wonderful it is that I am never alone. I bring my troubles to you and ask for divine strength to endure and the wisdom to handle it all.

Lord, I need never fear, even when someone sets out to harm me, for you are my stronghold. It does my heart good to think on your faithfulness.

Lord, I am between a rock and a hard place right now, so turn my rock into springs of water and I will be refreshed and renewed. Thank you for being with me through all this trouble. In the process, you are revealing things to me I would never have known otherwise.

You are King, and one day you will judge this world, so I can leave injustices for you to deal with. This sets me free from hate, bitterness, and anger. I am at peace in the midst of it all. I am strengthened to carry on. How amazing! How wonderful!

With a grateful heart, amen.

May the Lord give you success, and may he give you and your children success. May you be blessed by the Lord, who made heaven and earth.

—Psalm 115:14–15

Pamela Goss

Together We Are Strong

L ord, thank you for my children. They may not be perfect, but they are beautiful to me. Oh how they enrich my life. Together we are strong, like a cord that cannot be broken. Help me to bless them with my words, to build them up and to be an encourager.

Sometimes they head down a wrong path, which breaks my heart. Please help me to be understanding and compassionate and at the same time use wise discipline. Help me to do and say what is right even if it is hard. Give me courage and strength from your limitless power.

May each of my children come to know you in a personal way. May my life leave a wonderful example for them to follow. I claim your promise that my children's children will be blessed, that you will continue to work in their lives even after I am gone. The answer to the deepest needs of our hearts lies in having a relationship with you, Jesus.

You care about them even more than I do, so I place them in your hands of love. Richly bless, guide, and keep us, and make your face to shine upon us, for you abound in love and faithfulness.

In your name, my Jesus, amen.

I was in trouble, so I called to the Lord. The Lord answered me and set me free.

—Psalm 118:5

Pamela Goss

DAY TWENTY-THREE
Hope in the Dark

Oh Lord, I remember those times of despair when I longed to leave this world and be with you. Sometimes life seems too much to bear, all dark and hopeless and overwhelming. I feel rejected by others and even you seem far away from me. Everything I'm dealing with seems more than I can handle. Then, in your great mercy, you reached down, took hold of my hand, and pulled me out of that deep, dark pit. I realized that I have been in a serious depression, but in my state I couldn't see that. You guided me to get the help I needed, and I am thankful for the medications that exist to change this awful condition. Above all, I know you never left me. In fact, you were helping me all along.

Lord, you set me free! It feels like riding on the wings of an eagle, exhilarating and full of hope and joy. Taking my refuge in you gives me the victory. Fear is not my constant companion with you by my side. I rejoice this day because you shone your light into my dark pit and pulled me out. Oh how marvellous, wonderful, and great is your love for me. I am blessed to be your child. You are utterly trustworthy and my heart overflows with love for you.

In your precious name, Jesus, amen.

When I was in trouble, I called to the Lord, and he answered me.

—Psalm 120:1

Pamela Goss

True Freedom

Righteous judge, I cry out for justice. So many are suffering at others' hands, such as the many children who are being exploited and abused. My heart breaks for them.

I too had a rough childhood, facing much heartache and loneliness, and through you I have been able to forgive and leave the judgment of others to you. You are a righteous God and will do what is right. Forgiving sets me free from a life of hate and bitterness! You will right the wrongs so that I can live in forgiveness. I can leave the rest to you, especially when I have been forgiven of so much and have your Holy Spirit within to guide me. I am what I am by your grace. All the glory goes to you.

There are still those today who have set out to harm me, and I leave them to you. Only you can work in their hearts and lives. Hurting people will hurt people, so give me the strength to forgive quickly and get on with my life, for I have you on my side. I am your child, a child of the King and co-heir with Christ. I have it all when I have you. Praise the Lord! I shout with joy to my King! I sing praises to my wonderful Saviour. There is no one above you. Hallelujah!

In Jesus name who hears me, amen.

I was happy when they said to me, "Let's go to the Temple of the Lord."
—Psalm 122:1

Pamela Goss

DAY TWENTY-FIVE

In the Lord's Family

Lord, how I love to go to your house, to worship there, to sing songs of praise. I pray for our church. Make us one, loving, forgiving, and helping each other. Jesus, show me someone today who needs a helping hand. May I be a blessing, as I have so often been blessed. Lord, bless our leaders who are trying to shepherd us. Give them wisdom and protection from sin. Keep them strong. Show us ways to help them and be an encouragement in their ministry.

As we grow in Christ's likeness, may we reach out to those around us. Show us the way. I pray for peace among us, that any conflicts will be resolved. What a witness we would be for you if we always acted with love as our motive. I praise your name. Let your name be exalted on earth as it is in heaven. I praise you, my precious Redeemer and Friend.

In your name, Jesus, who loves me unfailingly, amen.

. . .put your hope in the Lord because he is loving and able to save.

—Psalm 130:7

Pamela Goss

DAY TWENTY-SIX
The Apple of His Eye

My shepherd, my heart is filled with love for you, for all you do for me every day. Every step I take is guided by you. No matter how small, I cast all my cares upon you and you hear me and help me. You wrap me in your comforting arms, helping me to bear up and survive. I am a survivor. My heart sings with praises to you.

God, you are so powerful and you do amazing things in my life. I can see now how the trials I've gone through have made me a better person. You care enough about me to work on me, to make me more like Jesus. My sin had put a wall between us, but now I am forgiven. Nothing can separate me from your love.

Oh how you love and care for me. You listen to me and give me such significance; I am your precious daughter, a princess, the apple of your eye, your beloved one. Your Holy Spirit fills me and keeps me. What a sweet fragrance this gives off, and I pray that others will be drawn to you through my life. Oh how greatly I am loved by you. You forgave me of all my sins and saved me from the pit of hell, now and forever. My hope is placed in you, my Saviour, for you hear me when I call and you answer in the most amazing ways. I love you, my Father.

In Jesus name, amen.

But I am calm and quiet, like a baby with its mother. I am at peace, like a baby with its mother.

—Psalm 131:2

Pamela Goss

Perfect Peace

Jesus, things right now are pretty scary and I am looking to you for deliverance out of these trials. But even if you don't deliver me right away, I trust you. My life is in your hands. I know I can live in perfect peace no matter what is happening around me, because I know that first of all these trials are chosen by your heart of love. My security lies in that. All things happen for a reason, so I accept the trials without bitterness, dispute, retaliation, or murmuring. I will not live in fear but love. May I be quick to forgive, slow to become angry, and careful with my words. May I show others the love you bestow on me so abundantly. Bless me in this, my Father.

I trust you to uphold my cause, to be my sovereign Lord and strong deliverer. All things are possible and you will make a way where there seems to be no way. You will not let me be burned in these fiery trials. It can only make me stronger. How awesome is that! Keep my mind focused on you, so that I know it is all being worked out in the best possible way. Your peace fills me as I rest in your loving arms. I love you, Lord.

In Jesus name, amen.

God, your thoughts are precious to me. They are so many! If I could count them, they would be more than all the grains of sand.

—Psalm 139:17–18

Pamela Goss

DAY TWENTY-EIGHT
Unconditional Love

Today, Jesus, my heart is filled with praises for you. Oh how marvellous it is that you, the Creator, look down from heaven and watch over me with such care and compassion. Angels stand guard around me and your Holy Spirit lives within me, giving me confidence and hope! So much love has been bestowed upon me. My deepest needs are met. I am complete in you, my Jesus. How amazing it is that the God of the universe has a purpose for my life, that I am thought of, wanted, loved, rejoiced over with songs, and delighted in. Hallelujah! My heart overflows.

May I always act in love and compassion. Because I am loved so unconditionally and abundantly, I have great security. Help me to pass on the goodness I receive, to be a blessing to those I meet today.

You showed your love for me by redeeming me, so that never again will anything or anyone be able to separate us. You didn't deserve to die on that cross, but you willingly and lovingly died for me. There is no greater love than that, to lay down your life. If you do nothing else for me, that is enough. That is the ultimate gift! How I love you! I will serve you all my days.

With a full heart, amen.

Let my prayer be like incense placed before you, and my praise like the evening sacrifice.

—Psalm 141:2

Pamela Goss

DAY TWENTY-NINE
A Faithful Friend

My precious Father, turn your heart towards me, your child, for my grief is consuming me. Hear my cries and come quickly to help me. The hurt runs so deep and my chest feels full of pain. I feel overwhelmed with all I have to deal with.

Lord, thank you for those you have sent to help me get through this. I thank you for my closest friend, who makes all things more bearable as she laughs and cries and prays with me. She is a treasure, a gift from you. May I too be a good friend, someone she can count on. Help me to be understanding and quick to forgive, just as you are to me. Help me to be not easily offended. How wonderful it is to have a kindred spirit!

Give me strength to face the day. Help me to rest in the knowledge that you have a plan for my life, and even though I can't see the solutions, you do. My life is in your hands. Bless us, as we seek to live for you.

With gratitude, amen.

The Lord is kind and shows mercy. He does not become angry quickly but is full of love.

—Psalm 145:8

Pamela Goss

Engraved on His Palm

L ord, you know what's on my heart. As I face this newest trial, it feels overwhelming and heart-breaking, but I know you are with me. I bring it to the foot of the cross and lay it down at your feet and trust you to work it all out for good. You are holy and just and all-powerful.

As I look back on other trials, I can see how you worked things out for the best. How wonderful it is that you love me so! I praise you, my Rock, my Defender, my Saviour, my Shield, and my Protector. You are my all in all. You are everything to me. I am so thankful for all your care of me. What a joy it is to be your child! Nothing and no one can snatch me out of your hand. Even more wonderfully, I am engraved on your palm. Oh how I love you! My praise for you is always on my lips.

In Jesus name, amen.

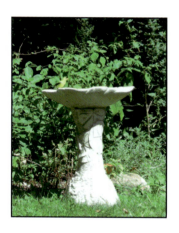

Praise the Lord! Sing a new song to the Lord; sing his praise in the meeting of his people.

—Psalm 149:1

Pamela Goss

A New Song

God, thank you for my new life, which is full and rich, with so many blessings! You saved me from a futile life, from making so many bad choices and ending up in a prison of my own making. Thank you for your goodness and mercy.

Just like being saved from drowning in stormy seas, you saved me. When I come to you, I am safe. Instead of saying "I don't need anyone," my trials have a way of bringing me to you. You are my all in all, my Rock, my King, my Creator, and my Provider. I kneel before you in worship. You are my shepherd and I am your sheep, and I will follow you all the days of my life.

I praise you for your faithfulness as I look back on my life. I remember the time when I was so sick and the doctors could do nothing more for me. My haemoglobin had dropped so low that it was life-threatening. Then, amazingly, I received a miracle of healing. You heard my cries, from the heart of a mother who wanted to look after her kids until they were grown. You understood my pain. I am so grateful for all that I have by being part of your family. Today I sing a song of joy! Praise the Lord! Praise the Lord!

In Jesus glorious name, amen.

Pamela Goss would love to hear from you.
Her email address is pamela31songs@gmail.com

Coming Soon

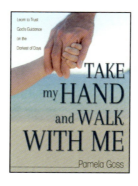

Take my Hand and Walk With Me
ISBN: 978-1-4866-1876-7

Sometimes along our journeys, we face a rough and rocky path. We cannot see clearly ahead and it's hard to keep persevering.

This is the time to take hold of God's right hand. He will travel with us, strengthening and guiding us, to a whole new destination—a place of abundance.

Come and discover the ways in which God will bless you when you take his hand in yours.